THE RULE OF 26

For Service-Based Businesses

Three Steps to Doubling Website Revenue

Michael Buzinski

Buzzbizz Media, LLC

Copyright © 2021 Buzzbizz Media, LLC

All rights reserved

No part of this book may be reproduced, or stored in a retrieval system, or transmitted in any form or by any means, electronic, mechanical, photocopying, recording, or otherwise, without express written permission of the publisher. Although the author and publisher have made every effort to ensure that the information in this book was correct at press time, the author and publisher do not assume and hereby disclaim any liability to any party for any loss, damage, or disruption caused by errors or omissions, whether such errors or omissions result from negligence, accident, or any other cause. Adherence to all applicable laws and regulations, including international, federal, state, and local governing professional licensing, business practices, advertising, and all other aspects of doing business in the US or any other jurisdiction is the sole responsibility of the reader and consumer. Neither the author nor the publisher assumes any responsibility or liability whatsoever on behalf of the consumer or reader of this material. Any perceived slight of any individual or organization is purely unintentional. Neither the author nor the publisher can be held responsible for the use of the information provided within this book.

ISBN- 9798744085148
ISBN-13: 9781234567890
ISBN-10: 1477123456

Cover design by: Buzzbizz Media, LLC
Library of Congress Control Number: 2018675309
Printed in the United States of America

CONTENTS

Copyright

Reviews

Testimonials

Dedication

PART 1	1
Should You Read This Book?	
My Promise to You	7
The Origin	9
Key Performance Indicators	15
Part 2	21
The Rule of 26 Defined	22
Increasing Unique Visitor Traffic	27
Increasing Conversion Rates	52
Increasing Average Revenue Per Client	70
Applying the Rule of 26	80
Wrap up	89
Part 3	92

The Next Step	93
Frequently Asked Questions	95
Helpful Resources	101
About Michael Buzinski	104
Buzzworthy Integrated Marketing	107
Small favor	109
Acknowledgements	110
Glossary	112
Bibliography	115

REVIEWS

"It [The Rule of 26] helped me understand what's truly important to focus on when it comes to my website. It's a needed book if you're serious about increasing your business through your website."

Michelle Traina
Business Owner/Coach

"I enjoy the concept of The Rule of 26 and find it to be straightforward and easy enough for any entrepreneur to understand. Breaking down each metric into bite sized pieces makes it easy for the reader to understand the road map and where to start."

Whitney DeBerry
Business Owner/Content Marketer

"I cannot believe how simple the Rule of 26 really is. The math checks out and I will be immediately implementing the Rule of 26 into my business. The book was easy to read, and I thought it offered a lot of value-packed strategies."

Aaron Contrall
Business Owner/Mortgage Broker

TESTIMONIALS

"Buzz" is a dedicated learner and focused professional. Because of his commitment to consistent learning and professional improvement you are dealing with an authentic professional. He has wonderful ideas for improving your business and provides you with the necessary tools to market your business while freeing up your time to make money. Do business with "Buzz" and you will be happy with the results."

Mark A. Grainger
Co-Founder & CMO Big Impact HQ

"Buzz [is] a valuable member of the digital marketing world with the vision and the tools to bring any creative project to life. His work is on point and demonstrates exceptional attention to detail .... His imagination and technical savvy make him well suited to the digital age. He is forward-thinking and brings passion and enthusiasm to his work. I would highly recommend Buzz to any organization's digital or marketing needs!"

Casey Kirby
Risk Management Consultant

DEDICATION

The Rule of 26 For Service-Based Businesses was inspired by and written with service-based business owners in mind, and thus dedicated to the same.

I am blessed to have served the marketing needs of over 750 businesses (as of 2021). I have the utmost respect for entrepreneur's dedication to their clients. It is my shared commitment to serving my clients that drove me to write this book.

It is my sincerest wish that your business flourishes from exposure to the Rule of 26. May it simplify the complexities of digital marketing in a way that frees you to keep focused on what you do best while growing your firm at the same time.

PART 1

WELCOME

SHOULD YOU READ THIS BOOK?

The purpose of this book is to leverage your time, energy, and money when it comes to marketing your website. I would be remiss if I didn't take the time to outline for whom this book is best suited. It would be an injustice for you to get halfway into this book and realize the Rule of 26 is not for you. To prevent you from wasting your time, I have outlined who should and who shouldn't read this book.

You should read this book...
1. If you are a **service-based business owner**, you should read this book. The primary purpose of this book is to help serviced-based businesses leverage their website to garner predictable qualified leads and earn a higher rate of return from each of those leads that

convert to new clients.

2. If you are already getting decent results from your website, but do not know how to double the current revenue it is producing, you should read this book. The Rule of 26 literally **doubles the income of any website**, **guaranteed**. I rarely, if ever, make guarantees with marketing, but with the Rule of 26, the math doesn't lie. Meet the three objectives of the Rule of 26 and you will double the revenue you are currently getting from your website.

3. You should read this book if you are an employee of a service-based business and have been tasked with digital marketing for your company. While the Rule of 26 is not a shortcut to success, it does break down the process of successful website marketing into terms non-marketing professionals can understand and execute. Reading this book is a great start to making a **drastic impact on your company's bottom line**. This will not only make your boss happy, but it could possibly get you a raise or even a promotion in the process.

4. If you are an established business with a healthy number of inbound sales coming from repeat clients and referrals and do not get many, if any, fruitful leads from your website. Yes, business is good, but what

would it look like to double your current sales? The Rule of 26 is a **force multiplier for successful businesses**. You have already done much of the hard work of creating a process to attract raving fans. Now plug that knowledge into the only sales asset that will work for you 24 hours a day, seven days a week, 365 days a year, without taking any sick days, or ever asking for a raise.

5. You have been successful for years with traditional advertising but have started to experience a dwindling return on investment (ROI) from your ad spend. While traditional media is still a viable option for many small to medium sized businesses (SMB), its effectiveness is significantly increased with a properly implemented website marketing strategy in place. The Rule of 26 **streamlines your website marketing strategy** by boiling your success down to three objectives.

You shouldn't read this book...
1. If you are an e-commerce or retail centric business owner, this is not the perfect book for you. While the Rule of 26 can work with any website, the strategies I cover in this book are geared specifically to service-based businesses. Instead, you should read books

specifically tailored to marketing products online.

2. If you are responsible for the marketing for a not for profit or non-profit organization, you will want to skip this book and read books that dive into attracting and cultivating volunteers and donors.

3. This book is also a pass if you are the CMO or marketing director for an enterprise-sized company. The Rule of 26 doesn't address the KPIs that pertain to the different objectives large corporations have compared to SMBs.

4. If you are a solopreneur without the time or resources to either execute or hire someone to execute the Rule of 26 for you. Marketing takes time and/or money regardless of how streamlined the strategy or simple the objectives. You can, however, read this book and get some wonderful ideas on how to make your website better. But until you dedicate time and/or resources to the process, you will fall short of the Rule of 26's true potential.

5. If you are not ready to take on 59% more clients than you are currently serving, you should put off reading this book. If you currently get most of your leads from your website and serve about 50 clients per month,

you need to be ready to serve about 80 clients. Regardless of your number, the worst thing you can do is surpass your capacity. It will ultimately result in bad customer service, low quality deliverables, and all the headaches that come with both. For now, I would suggest Mike Michalowicz's *Fix This Next*. When you feel you are ready to take on the influx of clients the Rule of 26 produces, then come back and we will get you rolling.

6. If you already know it all, are wildly successful with your digital marketing and have unlocked the key to scaling your business through website marketing. I passionately believe if it is not broken, do not try to fix it. I do, however, ask that you pass this book onto a colleague who is not as successful as you and keeps asking how to double revenue from their website.

To recap, you are reading the right book if you own or work with a small to medium-sized service-based business that wants to drastically increase the amount of revenue you garner from your website and are willing to put the resources required to follow through with the Rule of 26.

MY PROMISE TO YOU

If you have made it to this page, you have made a choice to invest the next two or so hours into your business's future. This is an awesome place for you to be right now. I know how valuable your time is and I will respect that. So, I make you these promises.

 A. I promise not to stuff the following pages with fluff. I am certain you have not bought this book to read my meandering stories of hope, triumph, failure, and redemption like most other books pad themselves with. Instead, I have written this book with just the good stuff. You know why you are here, and I know my system works, so we will forgo the dance and get to work.

 B. I promise to keep it simple. This is intended

for entrepreneurs without a marketing degree. I use as little digital marketing jargon as possible. I explain the buzzwords and acronyms I use with further explanation in the Glossary toward the back of the book.

C. I promise that if you follow the Rule of 26 and achieve its three straightforward objectives, you will **double your website revenue.** I put this in bold often because it is important to remember the impact doubling your revenue has on your business and furthermore, your life and quest for financial freedom.

D. My goal with this book is to arm you will the information you need to double your website revenue. To aid in that objective, you will have direct access to me by email at buzz@buzzworthy.biz. It is important to me that this book, while not a complete how to, gives you enough insight to take immediate action and be successful. Your questions will help both of us attain our goals. So, do not be shy and email me with your questions and/or thoughts.

THE ORIGIN

Did you know that service-based businesses account for 70% of all small to medium sized businesses (SMB), 99.7% of employing firms, and 64% all new private sector jobs in America[1]? That is an amazing fact, but tragically, nearly half of all small businesses will fail in the first five years[3]. Yet, there is extraordinarily little in the way of website marketing books or training to help them thrive and most SMBs lack the funds for done-for-you marketing services or to hire in-house talent. Yes, there are plenty of how-to books for specific tactics, but many are full of fluff and most fall short of solving the overall problem service-based businesses encounter when it comes to increasing revenue through their website.

This scenario troubles me deeply. See I have a *huge* soft spot for SMBs. I fervently believe they are the backbone of America's economy. As a small business owner, I understand the responsibility main street carries. The services and products we provide pale in comparison to the jobs we create, the dreams we fulfill, and communities we impact. With this in mind, I have accepted the responsibility to help as many entrepreneurs navigate the digital marketing landscape as I can. Educating business owners how to drastically increase their revenue and to realize their entrepreneurial dreams.

This is where the Rule of 26 comes in. See, for years, I focused on done-for-you marketing services for small to medium sized businesses. I grew my creative agency into a multimillion-dollar firm with a 13,000 square-foot facility serving over 300 companies across the United States every year. But with over 30 million SMBs in the US[4], I was barely scratching the surface.

In 2018, I reorganized my company to better focus my efforts and stay involved with what I love to do, marketing. The change meant a relatively miniscule footprint and more time to focus on my mission. Part of the journey included the need to radically simplify how I approached marketing objectives for my clients.

Up until the reorganization, my company followed the traditional advertising agency model of creating a customized strategy for each new client. This was time-consuming and expensive for the client. But every business has different needs, and the digital landscape becomes more convoluted every day, so it is a necessary evil right?

I finally asked myself, "Self, why does digital marketing need to be so complex for SMBs?"

Digital marketing is made complex by two main factors. The intricacies agencies create to measure success for large enterprises, and the plethora of tactics and tools available to obtain their marketing goals. Neither completely pertains nor scales down to the needs of SMBs, and less so for service-based businesses. Enter the Rule of 26.

The first step to developing the Rule of 26 was to eliminate all the unnecessary complexities of digital marketing as it pertains to non-enterprise businesses. This was not as hard to figure out as I thought it would be. The answer came from the question I heard the most over the previous 15 years. It is still one of the first questions new clients and entrepreneurs I meet during speaking engagements and networking events ask. You might have asked this same question a few times yourself and that is probably why you are reading this book.

Go ahead, ask it out loud. Seriously... out loud. If we are on the same page, you asked something like, "What is the simplest way to make more money from my website?"

It is alright if you asked a different question. It means you are at a different stage with your marketing. But sooner or later, every successful business owner turns to their website to earn more revenue. If you identify past this stage, then you are merely ready to take the Rule of 26 to stage two, which is to repeat the process (discussed in one of the last chapters of this book), or in your case, implement the rule.

In marketing, we must define goals and objectives as precisely as possible. Without a clear set of goals and objectives, a marketing campaign will run itself in circles (which many agencies count on to keep you on retainer). So, settling for "make more money" as our goal was too vague. To maintain simplicity, I decided to go with "double the revenue". Seems like a lofty goal for some, but, for true entrepreneurs, it is another day at the office, right?! Plus, it is an easy number to work with.

With a clear goal in place, it was time to find the simplest way to obtain said goal. But where to begin? Going back to the vision of this venture, I wanted to make the objectives as easy to measure and relatively obtain as possible. I also wanted a set of objectives that is easy to understand for everyone, regardless of their marketing expertise.

The outcome is a process that helps entrepreneurs who do not have the analytical knowhow or interest to understand layers of key performance indicators (the pros call them KPIs) that impact the bottom line.

Another level of the Rule of 26 was the ability for entrepreneurs to work with marketing professionals to help achieve the goal of doubling revenue from their website. I had to keep two basic types of business owners in mind.

First, there are the do-it-yourselfers. These are the overly busy entrepreneurs that have elected to manage their digital marketing on their own. They watch countless YouTube videos, listen to the hottest podcasts, and subscribe to an endless list of bloggers discussing the ins and outs of getting digital marketing. Every tidbit ingested promises to double, triple, or even ten-X the entrepreneur's revenue, seemingly overnight. The issue with trying to get information from so many sources is that if you do not understand the fundamental metrics that actually move the revenue needle, you can easily find yourself chasing new magical marketing unicorns every week. But, staring at way too many KPIs that don't really lead to large increases in sales is frankly a waste of time and money.

The second camp is the delegators. These more advanced entrepreneurs understand the power of enlisting the help of professionals to do what they are not good or passionate about doing. The danger of hiring marketing professionals lies in the fact that there are so many snake oil salespeople trying to peddle unrealistic outcomes. Now, do not get me wrong, there are plenty of wonderful digital marketing consultants and agencies out there. Unfortunately, in my experience, there are about three to four bad-to-mediocre ones to every great one.

Regardless of the indiviual digital marketer's ability, they must deal with the ups and downs of any campaign. So, when things go poorly, it is easy for the business owner to go on a journey of what

I call, 'chasing KPI waterfall' with their digital marketer. This can give the entrepreneur a false sense of progress in the wrong direction if they misunderstand the fundamental KPIs that are required to move a campaign back to profitability.

Whether you are part of camp one or two, the fact is that if you do not understand the fundamentals of digital marketing metrics, you can waste a lot of time, energy, and money trying to get more revenue from your website. For example, a widely used ecommerce platform called Shopify points out 67 KPIs to identify the progress of sales through your website. While the 67 they point out can be useful at some point in your strategic process, most all only created incremental increases. I found three core metrics that push your revenue substantially without needing to track dozens of confusing KPIs. Let us look at these three metrics that always count regardless of what new digital marketing widget, social media platform, or magical digital unicorn comes our way. Then I will show you how the Rule of 26 can help you double your website's revenue.

KEY PERFORMANCE INDICATORS

As I mentioned in the last chapter, Shopify identifies 67 KPIs that influence your digital marketing success. HubSpot, another client relationship manage (CRM) identifies anywhere between 15 and 28 KPIs (depending on which of their blog posts you read). While all these metrics can be helpful at different points in a business's life cycle, I found that most companies I encounter fall into the infancy stage of their digital marketing potential. For context, I consider a company spending less than $20,000 a month on website marketing to be the infancy stage and will benefit from focusing exclusively on these three KPIs: Unique Visitors, Conversion Rate, and Average Revenue Per Client (ARPC).

It is important to note that if you are working with a digital marketing agency or consultant/freelancer, you will get pushback from my last statement. This is to be expected. Digital marketers have been taught to look at early indicating KPIs and other metrics. Some use these kinds of numbers to justify less than stellar results and stagnant progress. It is acceptable for them to use these in their day-to-day methodology, but as you will see in coming chapters, all you are concerned with are Unique Website Visitors, Conversion Rate, and Average Revenue Per Client.

These seem self-explanatory to some, but just in case, I want to make sure we are all on the same page. If you are already a pro, feel free to jump to the next chapter, *The Rule of 26 Defined*.

Unique Visitors

The Unique Visitor KPI is defined as the number of individual users who visit your website, also known as unique traffic. For clarity, it is important to mention that there are two different flavors of traffic: unique (also referred to as new) and returning. For the Rule of 26, we are only concerned with the unique traffic. It is also important to note that to get actionable website traffic statistics, you will need to filter out bots and other inconsequential traffic that is not a live human. Otherwise, you will be working with fuzzy math and no one wants to work with inaccurate numbers when it comes to their bottom line.

The best place to find and track unique website traffic is Google Analytics. Ask your website designer for help with connecting analytics to your website. They can also help you filter the search bots and crawlers (what search engines use to search for content on the Internet), so your reports are accurate. If you built your own website or your designer is long gone and you can't do it yourself, email my team at support@buzzworthy.biz. We will connect your Google Analytics and set up filtering for you at no charge. Be sure to include "Rule of 26 Support" in the subject line so my team knows not to bill you.

Conversion Rate

The Conversion Rate KPI is defined as the percentage of conversions your site produces in relation to the amount of website visitors. A conversion is an action made by a visitor you feel contributes to revenue. Each business may have a different definition for this, but most will see a website conversion as a lead (visitor contacts company) from the website. For service-based businesses, this is normally making an appointment for a service, filling out a contact to receive information, or calling directly to the company. Others might only consider new business a conversion. Idetnifying with the latter is acceptable but brings in the complexity of your close rate (number of sales closed divided by the number of leads generated). For the purposes of the Rule of 26, I suggest considering any new contact from your website to your business as a conversion. Regardless of how you measure your conversion rate, it is important to stay consistent.

To calculate your conversion rate, divide the number of conversions by the number of unique website visitors in a defined period. So, if you see 20 conversions for every 1,000 unique visitors, your conversion rate will be 2%. The average conversion rate for websites vary between industries, but a quick Google search can give you a good number to start with. Otherwise, contact your marketing professional for precise trends.

As you might have started to notice, I like to keep things simple. When tracking conversions, I like to use click-to-calls and submitted forms works well. These measurements can be set up in your Google Analytics, which you have already set up to track unique website traffic, so you can see both in the same place. Again, if you need help, just email my team at support@buzzworthy.biz with "Rule of 26 Support" in the subject line.

Average Revenue Per Client

The average revenue of each client you obtain from engagement through your website over a prescribed amount of time is your Average Revenue Per Client or ARPC. For the Rule of 26, we look at the annual revenue from a client whether your work consists of one-off services or recurring billing, such as retainers. The easiest way to do this is to take your gross sales and divide it by the number of clients you serve per year. When looking for a multi-year average, be sure to calculate each year separately and then compute the average across the years. You will get an inaccurate number if you merely take total sales over multiple years and divide it by the total clients served over the same period.

An important factor to look at is the difference between your ARPC from web traffic versus other sources of sales. Most times this is awfully close if not identical, but if there is a large gap between them, you will want to be sure to only use the ARPC specifically from your website.

Now that we have identified the three KPIs you will use with the Rule of 26, it's time to dive into the rule itself and start working towards doubling your website revenue.

# PART 2

THE RULE OF 26

THE RULE OF 26 DEFINED

The Rule of 26 states:
"Increasing unique traffic, conversion rate, and ARPC by 26%, doubles website revenue."

That's it! It's really that simple. You double revenue just by increasing each of these KPIs by a mere 26%.

Don't believe me? Let me show you.

As seen in figure one on the next page, we start with a website getting 2,000 unique visitors with a 2.5% conversion rate and an ARPC of $1,000 garnering $50,000 in annual revenue. Simply increasing each of these by 26% literally doubles the revenue coming from your website. As you can see, it really is that simple! And keeping it simple is the name of our game.

Before the Rule of 26	Website Metric	After the Rule of 26
2,000	Unique Visitors	2,520
2.50%	Conversion Rate	3.15%
$1,000	Average Revenue Per Client	$1,260
$50,000	Revenue	$100,018.80

Figure 1: The Rule of 26 by the numbers

NOTE: *I suggest using monthly numbers when measuring unique visitors. Measuring changes in traffic monthly gives you enough time to see the results to any significant changes you make to your site. If you have a seasonal business, you will need to consider cyclical trends, so you are comparing apples to apples, year over year.*

A powerful attribute of this rule is that you can apply the rule repeatedly and the math doesn't change. Of course, at some point, you will need to bring in more metrics and different objectives, but entrepreneurs I have seen apply the Rule of 26 achieve their growth goals well before that is ever needed.

For argument's sake, look at figure one again. In the example to double website revenue, we only need another 520 unique visitors a month with a 0.65% bump in conversion rate and an added value of $260 average annual value per client.

If you run through the process again, your numbers are still extremely achievable. You are looking at 655 more unique visitors, another 0.82% increase in conversion rate, and adding $327 annual value to double your revenue *again*. Working the Rule of 26 *quadruple*s your annual revenue. Let that sink in for a second. Overall, this scenario only increased unique traffic by 58%, your conversion rate by 44%, and ARPC by $587 to increase revenue *four-fold*.

Think about what quadrupling your income would look like for you. What would that do for you as a person? How would it affect your family? What would it mean to your business? The Rule of 26 is all about achieving extraordinary gains through basic and realistic measures.

Now you might be asking, "Sure, the objectives have been simplified, but how hard is it to achieve each of these objectives?" That is a great question. The answer will depend on a multitude of variables such as...

- How long have you had your website?

- What do your current metrics look like?

- What are you currently doing to drive more traffic to your site?

- Are your KPIs below, at, or above industry standards?

- The list goes on.

Dwelling on how hard achieving these objectives are, will get us nowhere. Believe it or not, you have already overcome the hardest part of digital marketing, identifying profitable objectives. There are thousands of service providers and widgets that tout outstanding results. But without a clear understanding of which KPIs directly affect your bottom line you'll end up spinning your wheels wasting time, energy, and money. I have tested hundreds of new shiny objects over the years. I have journied countless rabbit holes through social media pop-ups, Google search results, and YouTube ads searching for answers to make websites a reliable source of qualified leads. I found that no single widget or tactic multiplies revenue by itself. The Rule of 26 is impactful because it doesn't rely on gimmicks, only plain math.

If you think about it, you now have a simple road map to success. Now it's time to start exploring the different routes to obtaining the success you are looking for. Let's dive into how to successfully ac-

complish each of the three Rule of 26 objectives.
Let the heavy lifting begin.

INCREASING UNIQUE VISITOR TRAFFIC

The quality of your website traffic data is the first and foremost detail you *must* attend to. Google analytics can be as much of an honest friend as a bold-faced liar. In marketing, we have a saying, "Garbage in, garbage out." Starting with inaccurate data will create a world of headaches and confusion as you progress through the Rule of 26 objectives.

With that said, before you move forward with any tactic I cover in the upcoming chapters, it is imperative you confirm your website traffic reports reflect unique human visitors as accurately as possible. The simplest approach to keep bot traffic filtered out of your Google Analytics reports is to use Google's automatic filter. Simply set up this filter by going to your view settings and click the box that says, "Exclude all hits from known bots and spiders." This doesn't preclude all erroneous traffic from populating your report, but it gets us close enough for this particular intention.

If you do not know how to navigate Google Analytics, talk with your webmaster or digital marketing service provider. If neither of those are an option or not able to deliver the reports you need, my team is available by email at support@buzzworthy.biz. Be sure to put "Rule of 26 Support" in the subject line so they know not to bill you for this complimentary service.

Now that you have filtered out the commonly known search engine bots and crawlers, what does your monthly unique visitor traffic look like? Are you working with less than 10,000? Maybe less than 1,000. If you are looking at less than 500, you are not alone. According to the Search Engine Journal, "Over 50% of local business websites receive less than 500 visits per month[6]." The good news is that a 26% increase of 500 is a bit easier than that of 10,000. Either way, reaching 26% is extremely attainable. Let's look at a few tactics that can get you there.

Earned Traffic

Earned traffic is website traffic you don't directly pay for, but rather earn through time and energy. The most direct way to earn traffic is networking. Networking can be as simple as telling your friends and family about your website. That might sound kind of salesy or weird, but your inner circle can be the most productive referral sources at your disposal.

When approaching this kind of conversation, start with a simple question like, "Who do you know who needs help with [*insert the problem you solve*]? If your service helps people, then you are not selling anything, and your friends and family are not pushing anything. You are merely helping people with an issue they have.

Reaching beyond your immediate circle of influence will involve attending business and charity functions, business networking events, social gatherings, and the like. Be sure to always have business cards with your website clearly printed on it at all these events. I can't tell you how many times over the years I've been asked for a business card at a non-business-related event with nothing to offer. How embarrassing is that? A marketer without their marketing tools at hand.

Speaking of marketing tools, there is a long-game tactic I have used over the years that has produced surprising results – pens. Yes, old fashion pens, nothing cutting edge and definitely not an original idea, but I do it in a particular way that focuses on website traffic.

Instead of round pens, like most others, I would buy tri-sided Bic balled-point pens with something printed on all three sides. On one side, was my business name, the second side my slogan, and the third my website address. Why not my phone number, you ask? For two reasons. First, visiting a website is much less committal. People are a lot less likely to call a company they don't know much about or have a clear understanding of what they do. But they will spend a couple of minutes visiting a website. The second reason is that when they inevitably lose the pen, they are more likely to remember the website name over your phone number.

I always kept at least two or three of my pens with me everywhere I went. When at restaurants, I would swap out the cheap pen they left in the billfold with mine. I would whip one out when someone randomly needed one and then told them to keep it. I'd even leave them on counters where I signed credit card slips for purchases.

I only used this pen technique for about 18 months before I started seeing my pens turn up in restaurants I hadn't left pens at before. This meant my pens were getting circulated along with my business name, slogan, and website address. When I asked new clients where they heard of me, I started hearing stories of how they used my pen at a restaurant and looked up my website out of curiosity. I even had a couple of clients keep the pen and had it with them at our first meeting.

Don't fret if getting out and networking or leveraging your inner circle isn't up your alley. There are a few other ways to earn website traffic. Let's start with email marketing.

Email List

If you haven't used email marketing to build a following yet, you are missing out. A 2019 study by DMA Marketer found that you can expect a $42 return on every $1 invested in email marketing[7]. To put it another way, each email address on your list should garner $1 in sales per month. If you have 1,000 emails, you should be garnering at least $1,000 per month from your list, $10,000 for 10,000 emails, and so on.

The obvious way to increase the value of your email list is to create a call to action (CTA) in each of your emails. This CTA doesn't have to be a sales pitch every time. Instead, send your readers to your website anytime you update information, or add a new team member, or have a new upcoming event. The objective is to only give enough information in each email to entice readers to click through to your website for more information.

There are many email marketing platforms out there. Some start out free like Mail Chimp. Unforunately, those that start free don't scale with your business well. For the best value and easiest-to-use features, I recommend Constant Contact. The setup is easy, the interface is user friendly, and they offer loads of options to leverage your email list.

I have been working with Constant Contact since 2006 and offer a complimentary setup and walk-through for anyone who signs up through my partner link. Just email support@buzzworty.biz to get started.

Social Media

You probably already use social media in some form or fashion in your life. And if you are like most business owners, your company leverages it at some level for marketing. Social media doesn't quite have the same potency as email marketing, but it is free (for the most part), and you should continue using it if you currently get any degree of success from it.

If you are not big on social media and don't currently have a sizable following, you should stay away from spending a lot of time getting started now. It is much easier and more lucrative to grow a profitable email list than a valuable social media following. The main reason is engagement. A post on Facebook is likely to be seen by 6% of your fans compared to an average of 18% of your subscribers opening your email[11].

When using social media, be diligent about pushing your fans to your website for all the reasons you would email your list. Be careful to keep a healthy balance between engaging conversation and pitching. On average, you should only be pitching one out of every five posts on each social media channel you use. Remember, you can send your social media followers to your site for reasons other than buying your service, so be creative.

Backlinks And Referrals

Backlinks are website links from other websites back to yours. These links can come from strategic referral partners you may have or through an affiliate program you have created to incentivize people to drive traffic on their site to yours. You can also reach out to businesses with complimentary products or services to yours and ask if they would be interested in linking to your website. One of the simplest backlinks you can get are from directories and search engines like YP.com, Google Maps, and Yelp just to name a few.

Sometimes you will need to be a bit creative with where to get backlinks. The goal is to get people who will ultimately be interested in hiring you for your services to see your site. Getting a link on a website that doesn't get viewed by your target marketing is quite useless, so having a few strategic links is much better than a plethora of low-quality links.

High-quality backlinks aren't always easy to find. Frank, one of my clients with the unique service of driving rented moving trucks for families, needed help getting more traffic to his site in new markets. His website was already getting great traffic and the site's content was all but maxed out. I decided to look for blog sites that talked about real estate and relocation. I found a few great bloggers that had a monthly following of over 25,000. I was able to get these bloggers to write about this unique service on their blog and include a link back to Frank's website.

That single blog generated over 500 visits in the first month. Since the blog resides on the bloggers site for the foreseeable future, it will garner new traffic every month. This is free traffic from visitors already interested in the topic related to my client's service.

Speaking Events & Webinars

There are plenty of ways to get in front of groups of people. Some examples include guest speaking at business and social clubs, associations, podcasts, webinars, and radio shows. Anytime you get a chance to speak in front of your demographic, have a plan to plug your website. Better yet, coordinate with your host to have them plug it for you with a possible incentive for their specific audience.

The key to speaking events is the call to action at the end of your presentation. Get people excited about contacting you. Don't squander this opportunity. I have a client who's been with me since 2006 that came from a short 15-minute presentation. My call to action pertained to getting people to stop wasting money in the Yellow Pages phone book. My complimentary 30-minute consultation offer in 2006 has resulted in over $360,000 of services rendered (as of 2021). Since working with them, my client's company reached over $11 million in annual revenue and is one of my best friends.

Another big opportunity is webinars. Now, the word 'webinars' makes some people uneasy. It brings visions of a big hassle, lots of pre-production and months of preparation. Webinars can be as simple as a PowerPoint presentation and a microphone with a simple screen recording software like Screencastify or recording yourself in a video teleconference meeting room like Zoom. The only other thing you need is a topic your target audience would be interested in. Give the topic a title and start utilizing the resources like social media, networking, and email marketing to invite people. The best part of webinars is that you can automate webinars to attract and engage top-of-funnel prospects (tire-kickers).

One of my mortgage broker clients, Aaron, is a great example of how to use an auto-webinar to both get more website traffic and free up time in the sales process. He and his partner were getting bogged down with answering the same questions from prospective buyers calling into the office over and over. The question-and-answer sessions are essential to the sales cycle in the mortgage industry, but new homebuyers would rather call into the office than drudge through a Frequently Asked Questions (FAQ) page on some website to find answers. So, Aaron created an event out of the exercise and now uses it as both a time-saving tool for new clients and a lead generation tool with his email marketing, social media marketing, networking, and more.

Press Releases

Utilizing the media is an effective way to get word out about your business to a large audience, for free. Press releases are a short compelling news story submitted to media outlets like TV, radio, and newspaper/websites. The purpose is to pique the media's attention enough to compel them to do a story on you. If you have created something that you feel is newsworthy, then a press release is a free avenue for getting the word out.

Start with your local news outlets and work out from there. You can also look at community calendars or even long form posts for business or related interest groups on social media. Once you get one story broadcasted, exploit it by getting recordings of the audio or video (or links) and share it on social media, email, and any other avenues you have. There are plenty of templates on the Internet to help you fashion the press release format.

Search Engine Optimization

Search Engine Optimization (SEO) is the art and science of getting your website link placed on the first page of search engine results pages (SERP). The art is finding the keywords and phrases people commonly use to find your type of service. The science is understanding and leveraging the everchanging algorithms of search engines like Google. The outcome is high amounts of inbound website traffic of people actively looking for your services.

Since SEO is so powerful, you might be asking why I listed it last on this abbreviated list. I do value SEO tremendously because it accounts to over 50% of traffic around the web. Those who rank on the first page are getting over 90% of all organic search engine traffic[12]. It also drives 1,000 times more traffic to websites and is 14 times more profitable than social media[12]. But, if you notice, the list has been presented in the shortest and easiest to longest and hardest paths to increasing your website traffic. SEO is a long game that takes a lot of patience and diligence mixed with knowhow. Another reason I put SEO last is because traffic begets site authority which is a factor in your search engine rankings. So, the more you can do through direct traffic strategies, the less work and the quicker you will move up on search engine rankings. I won't go through how to do SEO here, but I will give you some quick tips on things to look at when executing SEO.

➢ Pay attention to your site load speed. Sites that load slower than 2.5 seconds are more susceptible to visitors leaving before the content loads. That is why Google looks down on slower loading websites and takes away site authority for it.

➢ Website metadata stored in your website's code. Metadata is used by search engines to understand what each page portrays on your site. Optimizing your metadata and making sure your current sitemap is submitted to Google is an easy way to increase your Google Juice.

➢ Ensure your content is readable for those with disabilities by making your website ADA compliant. There are free sites that will scan your site for accessibility. A quick search on Google will give you a few current options to do it yourself or have your web developer upgrade your site. This is a relatively quick fix, that shouldn't cost more than $200 for most small websites.

➢ Use profitable keywords appropriately. Not enough density will hurt your ranking just as much as too much, or what is called keyword stuffing. You need to mention your most profitable keywords enough for the bots to recognize your page is focused on a particular topic without diminishing the user experience.

➢ Mobile optimization is a key component to

getting your website onto the first page of any search engine. Mobile optimization looks at the load speed on mobile devices along with the user experience of your site on a cell phone. You will likely need a major overhaul of your website if it is more than five years old and you don't have a webmaster keeping its mobile responsive coding current.

Paid Traffic

The fastest way to get traffic to your website is utilizing paid traffic. Paid traffic comes in many forms both on and off-line. For the purposes of this discussion, I am going to focus on Internet options because they are normally more affordable, flexible, and the most accurate when tracking traffic and effectiveness.

It is extremely important to have your conversion process working smoothly before you launch any paid advertising campaign. The worst thing you can do is throw money into a campaign and bleed potential clients due to an inadequate conversion process. A couple of items on your website to check are your forms and phone numbers.

All of your website forms should be tested for usability and sent to an email or CRM that is actively monitored. The last thing you want a conversion to do is wait or get lost in the ether of undelvierable emails or unattended CRM funnels. It is best that mulitple people outside of your office check this for you. Be sure to get their feedback on the process of filling out forms and any other hoops you make prospects go through to get in touch with you. In my opinion, it is best to create as few barriers to connect as possible. Make your forms short by asking for only the most pertinent information needed to follow up.

Check your entire site for any mention of a

phone number. Make sure each instance is click-to-call enabled for mobile devices. If you have mulitple departments, use direct lines to indivual departments when able. The more streamlined and easy you make it for potential clients to talk with someone who can help the better.

Now that your site is ready, let's look at paid traffic tools.

Paid Search

Google AdWords is the big dog when it comes to paid search engine ads and, in my opinion, the most effective avenue when it comes to paid traffic. There are two advantages to Google Ads. First, you are working with a platform where potential customers are actively searching for what you have to offer. Second, if you elect for pay-per-click (PPC) ads, you only pay for ads when a user clicks on your ad. The link in your ad will usually go to your website so you always get something for your money. Best case scenario, you get a new client. Worst case, you gather useful information on how to make your website convert visitors better. The catch here is that Google Ads are not easy to set up and to get the best results, you will want to enlist professional help.

Youtube

YouTube is the second largest search engine in the world after Google. What makes YouTube ads appealing is that they utilize video to help you tell your story. The spectacular thing about YouTube is that you can choose where and how your ads are placed. Conquesting pre-roll ads is my go-to. Conquesting is when I place ads in front of competitors' videos with a five to ten-second uninterruptible segment before their video starts. Even if the viewer doesn't click through at that moment, your brand still makes an impression and can help with top-of-mind awareness.

You will run into two hurdles with YouTube Ads. The first challenge is creating a video, which can be a daunting task for some. It is easy to find professionals that can help you with getting something that will work for as little as $100. The best places to start are platforms like UpWork, or Fiverr. You only need a 15-second spot, and it doesn't have to be a big production. Start by shooting a quick explainer video using your smartphone and then having a professional polish it up, add graphics and text as needed.

Your second challenge will be managing your YouTube campaign, which is much like managing a PPC campaign. So, unless you have the time and money to experiment with this platform, I suggest hiring a professional with specific experience managing YouTube Ads to help you. It *is* an added expense, but the return on investment will be better in the long run.

Social Media Advertising

I have been helping business owners with social media since 2005, or some would say, since the dawn of social media. I found that most entrepreneurs fall into one of three camps. They don't know anything about monetizing paid social media, have no interest in learning how to run paid social media campaigns, or both. If any of these are you, please keep in mind that *good* campaign managers are not cheap, so you will need to have an ad budget of over $1,500 per month to make it worth your while.

Regardless of whether you do it yourself or with a consultant, you will have a few options to choose from when dealing with social media advertising. Most platforms offer options with photos, videos, carousel, stories, and/or moments. The landscape for social media advertising is constantly changing, so it is important to keep your fingers on the pulse of the industry when engaging in paid social media. The other option is to rely on your digital marketing manager to keep you in the know.

Website Sponsorships

A great way to get in front of your potential customer is finding a popular website that your target market frequents and is complimentary to your service. Say you're a physical therapist. Your target audience will be those who want to be mobile, right? So, find a popular local or regional website that promotes a healthy and active lifestyle. Contact the owner of the site and ask if they are interested in selling ads on their website. An advantage of this avenue is the cost is usually fixed and the ads will be served to users that will be more likely interested in your service than on broader advertising channels. This is kind of like AdWords without all the research and campaign management.

Third-Party Ad Networks

When you are ready to advertise on several websites your target audience is using in their day-to-day lives, you will need to find an agency that offers a third-party ad network. Third-party ad networks connect advertisers to websites that are willing to host advertisements. Placement involves intense algorithms between several servers that allow your ads to be precisely placed in front of a laser focused audience. How focused you ask?

I took on a political action committee (PAC) for a state senator campaign as a client a few years ago. The PAC was interested in adding digital marketing to the traditional door knocking and direct mail campaigns of old. I knew social media would be on top of their list, but I changed their view of digital ads once I showed them third-party ad networks. I was able to pinpoint the IP addresses of everyone on their mailing list. The list was comprised of every voter registered with the same party affiliation and within the candidate's district. Once a user saw an ad at home, the campaign would tag their phone which would then trigger more ads as they were out and about throughout the day.

The candidate won and credited my client's campaign efforts to helping with the victory. The crazy part of it all is that the digital ad campaign cost significantly less than their direct mailers and I delivered well over ten times the frequency to their target audience.

Most people do a mix of paid and earned traffic to increase their unique visitor count. It is important to remember that for your first time applying the Rule of 26, you are only looking to increase traffic by 26%. So, if your site averages say 1,000 users per month, you are only needing 260 more monthly users than you are currently getting. This means you do not have to put the pedal to the medal to be successful. You can easily get this from just one of any of the options I covered.

INCREASING CONVERSION RATES

Let's start this chapter with setting reasonable expectations. First thing to consider is that conversion rates vary from industry to industry and between different types of websites. In 2021 the average conversion rate across all industries range between 2.35% and 5.31%[13]. The lowest converting sites are eCommerce sites (online product sites) at 1.84% and mobile app store pages rank the highest with an average of 26.4%[13].

For our purposes I will use the lower end of the overall average. Using the Rule of 26, our goal will be to increase your conversion rate of 2.35% by 26%. That's only 0.611% and very doable, right? Right!

Increasing conversion rates can be a very

mystical science for many. It involves a little psychology mixed with user experience design, good copy, and a dash of luck. Notice none of the ingredients are quantitative? That's what makes the mystery so confounding. We are trying to use qualitative measures to create quantitative results. So, in the execution we sometimes hit it out of the park on the first swing at one site and then left scratching our heads on the next. It's a tale of two websites and it happened to me.

I have worked with quite a few dentists over the years. It is an extremely competitive market. Dr. Brent was the first dentist I ever worked for. He was going through a change of guards, if you will, with the 20-year veteran dentist retiring and Brent taking over the clinic.

As one would guess, the retiring dentist was a bit traditional in his ways and thus his website was sorely lacking. So, I did what any self-respecting digital marketer would do, and redesign the entire site. Awesome, right? Well, mostly. The site started performing 100-times better than the old site in every KPI, even the average conversion rate. But the conversion rate was still a bit low for their industry.

Looking over the user data, I noticed that the page with the most views was the "About the Doctors" page. That isn't uncommon but, peculiarly, it was also the highest exit page. This means people were coming to this particular page and leaving without converting. Why? We had a call to action at the bottom inviting visitors to make an appointment, the doctors' profiles were personable, and pictures attractive and professional. What was missing?

I noticed we had a "new patient" special on many other pages across the site, but it wasn't on this page. At first, I didn't feel that it would be necessary because the glowing profiles would be enough to entice users to make an appointment. Obviously, I was wrong. So, I decided to test the "new patient" offer on that page. Seemingly overnight conversions shot up well beyond our goals. I looked like a genius!

A few years later I worked with another retiring dentist. This time, the doctor didn't have a successor and wanted to find a buyer. Our first goal was to increase the perceived value of practice by drastically increasing his number of patients. No sweat.

This time, the client's website was nice and didn't seem to need too much attention. The conversion rate was decent, but the monthly traffic was less than optimal for our objectives. Traffic is an easy fix, so we went to work and pushed out some social media ads, Google Ads, and integrated some radio ads.

Traffic immediately shot up, but conversely, and strangely, the conversion rate dropped off. This isn't a common issue, and I was a bit baffled by the conundrum. I went through my bag of tricks one by one, and nothing was making a significant enough change. Then I started looking deeper into the website visitor demographics. I compared the new visitors to the client's existing patient demographics. There was a mismatch. The doctor had a loyal but aging patient list, and the advertising was attracting a younger audience.

Once I made this distinction, the solution was obvious, and we immediately went to work updating the website's content. With a fresher and younger voice, the conversion rate increased substantially. My client grew his practice over 50% in a matter of 12 months and sold for more than expected within two months of his target date.

These are just two examples of how identifying the solution to sluggish conversion rates can be tricky. There is no black and white solution. The winning answer in both scenarios could have just as easily failed for various reasons and that's where the "dash of luck" comes in.

The most significant activity you can do to decrease the need for a dash of luck is to identify the right audience for your website. See, not all traffic is good traffic. For example, say you are offering the best dentures in the state, what good is there to drive young families to your site? Not a lot, huh? You can easily increase your conversion rate by just driving better traffic to your website without touching anything I am about to show you.

Your first step is to refine who you are attracting to your website during the 'increasing traffic' objective. If your visitors match with your perfect client's profile, you are ready to move onto increasing your conversion rate. Here are a few areas which will help you achieve this objective.

Content

Content will be your first concern. As you saw in my second example, what you say on your website can have a big impact on your conversion rate. The first mistake most service providers make is talking about themselves and their team over the needs of the potential client.

The entire point of your website is to connect the right visitor with a solution to a problem or desire *they* have. Your ideal client is concerned about their needs, so you need to speak to them through the lens of those needs. Read through your homepage and see if you loaded the content with self-accolades and promotion. Building yourself up has its place, but it should come after compelling content that speaks directly to your potential client's situation and shows you can solve their problem or satisfy their desire.

The key to creating converting content is to tailor your verbiage specifically to your ideal client. Paint the picture of what they look like, both physically and emotionally. Where are they in life? What are their struggles? What do you offer that would make their life better? How does your service change their life?

Avoid being a generalist. If your target is anyone or everyone, you get a picture of no one. It's been my experience that it is hard to sell anything if you are talking to no one. Additionally, if you are honest with yourself, you don't really want to talk with or serve just anyone. Not all business is good business and I know I hate wasting time with unqualified prospects and even worse, bad clients. So, the more specific your content is to your ideal client, the more likely you are to convert the best prospects.

Once you have connected with the perfect client, be clear with your service's value proposition. Why should they work with you over your competitors? What makes you different. Your difference doesn't have to be worlds apart from your competitors. One degree of separation makes you unique. If you only have that one degree, magnify it, and show how that one distinction makes all the difference.

User Experience

How your website is laid out will dictate whether a user sticks around to connect with you or not. User Experience (UX) is the science of examining how users use your website and optimizing underperforming user flow. There are some free tools like hotjar.com that will literally show you where visitors hang out on your site, how long it takes to click on certain buttons, and where on pages they exit the site. Using tools like this can make optimization of UX much easier than just staring at exit page results and other vague website metrics.

The overall aesthetics of your site is also important. I have been known to say that good content is more important than good looks, but you can bet that if you have something that appeals to your audience visually, it will attract more engagement than good content alone. Starting with the right colors can make a big difference in the effectiveness of your site. Your logo should be the anchor to your website's color scheme. Finding complimentary colors to help convey a certain personification of your brand helps keep your message synchronous with your content.

Here are some examples of what messages colors can express.
- **Black:** edgy, sophisticated, alluring
- **White:** client, healthy, wholesome

- **Gray:** somber, formal, established
- **Blue:** trustworthy, soothing, enticing
- **Green:** growing, flourishing, natural
- **Brown:** rustic, masculine, stout
- **Red:** hostile, critical, spirited
- **Orange:** active, playful, affordable
- **Yellow:** kind, happy, watchful
- **Pink:** feminine, spry, intimate
- **Purple:** luxurious, royal, sexual

You've likely heard the phrase, "A picture is worth a thousand words." That's why using inviting and relevant imagery on your website is a wonderful way to increase the user experience. Images can be photographs, graphics, infographics, and graphs to name a few. When used correctly, good imagery can take a ho-hum page to a high-performing page overnight.

Now that you have the visitor's attention, it is time to get them to engage with your site. The objective is to get them clicking deeper into your site. The more they click, the more likely they are to convert. There is an art to engagement though. Making users click just for click's sake is a surefire way to push potential clients away.

Here are some simple tactics to keep your audience engaged:

➢ Respect the visitor's time and get straight to the point of how you can make their life better. In general, you have about eight seconds to grab a new visitor's attention and get them to engage with the site before they bounce to the next website. Use brief and enticing introductions to complex topics and then invite the user to click through to a subpage to learn more.

➢ Overcome standard objections within your content. This reduces the friction of the conversion process and overcomes the most common reasons people don't engage further before the visitor has a chance to think of them.

➢ Answer questions to frequently asked questions regarding your service. The better you can show that you understand their needs before they even have a chance to ask them, the faster you will build their trust in you.

➢ Just like in any sales situation, at some point you must ask for the sale. Your call to action can come in many different flavors. You can go for the hard sell and use scarcity to drive your visitor to act now. Maybe the slow route with a free teaser offer is your speed. Whatever flavor you use, be succinct with your offer and be sure you have built enough value to compel action. Start by placing your call to actions anywhere you would have a soft or hard close in a conversation with a prospect.

➢ Getting a user to engage with a call to action can easily be undone with a difficult submission process. Service providers largely use some sort of form to gather information from the user in exchange for some form of free information or to schedule an appointment. In either scenario, make this process as quick and easy as possible. You only need enough information to deliver the free offer or return the inquiry. Use the K.I.S.S. method: Keep It Super Simple.

Social Proof

In the simplest of terms, social proof is evidence that others who look like your target audience approve of your service or product. Testimonials are the most common way entrepreneurs use social proofing. Testimonials can be collected via social media, directly from your website, follow-up emails after a purchase, or personal invitations from the service provider. You can use written, audio, and/or video testimonials to help show visitors that you are who you are, and your product delivers how you promise.

There are other social proof widgets you have likely seen hovering around the bottom of the screen. They usually come in a pill shaped container touting person after person who has signed up for a service or is attending an event. These play on our inherent herd mentality. If a lot of people are doing it, it must be good.

The premise of social proof is to portray a sense of community. Sharing the journey of your company is just as much a social proof tactic as sharing the stories of your clients. Be human, be relatable, and be approachable. These traits are unique to service-based businesses, which creates a competitive advantage between similar service providers. People do business with people they like and trust. Share what your perfect clients like about you and your business through testimonials and other social proof tactics. Social proof is a trust-building exercise. The more you share, the more people will trust your brand.

Chatbots

A chatbot is a computer program that essentially replicates human dialogues. It facilitates interaction between a human and a machine the interaction, which occurs via messages or voice command. A chatbot is coded to work autonomously without a human operator.

The use of chatbots can be both a time and cost saver. They are also a wonderful sales automation tool. Studies show up to a 30% savings in customer service and support costs[14]. Chatbots have become a go-to for increasing conversions for several reasons.

Chatbots work 24-hours a day, seven days a week. They never take a sick day, never ask for a raise, and never complain. Chatbots cost a fraction of the salary and resources a human representative requires and can answer up to 80% of the frequently asked questions potential clients ask[15]. I have several clients who take advantage of my company's chatbot. In every instance, they have told me how many fewer unqualified calls they get. This gives them more time to work with qualified prospects and better customer service to existing clients.

When I set up chatbots for my clients, I work through a self-qualifying process while answering the user's questions. Chatbots are especially effective for high-valued services like my lawyer clients. By qualifying website visitors through a chatbot, I have reduced unqualified calls into their offices by as much as 60%. This allows in-house assistants to answer more calls before they go to voicemail. Ultimately, chotbots facilitate better customer service and more opportunities to schedule qualified leads from your website.

Continuity

Regardless how visitor's land on your website, be sure what you said to get them there matches what they see upon arrival. No one likes a bait and switch, and integrity is all you have for a first impression; so, don't squander this single opportunity. An example of taking continuity to the next level is having a separate website for differing demographics that speaks directly to their independent needs, talks to their unique pain points, and builds value to their specific point of view.

One of my CPA clients had a large core team with several specialties. They developed a Google Ad campaign that produced a high number of click-throughs but noticed a lagging conversion rate. I quickly noticed they had set up all ads sets to land on their homepage which immediately bombarded visitors with a plethora of solutions that didn't correlate with their issue. I re-organized all ad and backlinks to land pages specific to the issue the referring link pertained to. The site produced an immediate spike in conversions.

Potential clients are looking for solutions. Anything you do to confuse the process in solving their problem will push them away. Keep your visitors comfortable through every step of their website journey with continuity and consistency.

Close Rate

I briefly mentioned at the beginning of the book, that some entrepreneurs only consider a conversion from their website a closed sale. This ties your website conversion rate to your close rate, thus directly affecting the same. This reminds me of Joanne, a business coach I worked with. She focused the value of her marketing efforts solely on new business. When we started working together, Joanne's website didn't give her many chances to close business, if any. After deploying a series of website conversion tactics her number of appointments rose steadily. She was remarkably busy on sales calls every week but wasn't seeing a significant increase in sales.

Looking deeper into the situation we uncovered the underlying issue. We increased her traditional website conversion rate to 5% but her close rate was only about 10%. So, effectively, she only realized a 0.5% "conversion rate". I knew I could drive more quality traffic to her site, but unfortunately, she couldn't take more sales calls during her day and service more new clients. So, we focused on two objectives. First, we aimed to qualify website visitors better before allowing them to make an appointment, effectively reducing the number of sales calls. Second, we worked on her offering and off-line closing process.

Two months later, we saw a decrease of website conversions down to 2.7% and an increased close rate of 25%. This gave us an effective conversion rate of 0.65%, which is a 35% increase. With 50% less sales calls, we could choose to increase traffic. But the better bet was to fine-tune the quality of conversions even further and continue increasing her close rate. Eventually, Joanne achieved a 40% close rate with the same 2.7% website conversion rate bringing her effective conversion rate to 1.08%. That made her incredibly happy.

Coming from a miniscule number of leads to 2.7% average conversion rate was a huge deal for Joanne. But as you see, just increasing calls to the office wasn't the answer. Had she come to me with the same website statistics as we concluded with, solely increasing her close rate from 10% to 25% would produce a 150% increase in her effective conversion rate. That's one and a half times the revenue by just increasing her close rate by 15%.

Increasing conversions fundamentally comes down to making it as easy for your visitor to say yes to your offer as possible. The more hurdles you created for the visitor, the more work you create for yourself and your marketing team. The best tool is to get feedback from your users, both buying and not. Focus on what your buyers loved about their experience and steer away from what drove the others to bounce from your site.

INCREASING AVERAGE REVENUE PER CLIENT

A plethora of books are out there that cover the art of milking your client for more money at the point of the sale. While many have good intentions, my perspective focuses on win-win situations throughout the transaction. My philosophy in increasing the average value of each client is based on creating more value *for* the client. When you find an honest way to do this, you will have raving fans for life with crazy repeat customers and high referral rates. Here are the core practices I use to increase the average revenue per client (ARPC).

Bill What You Are Worth

I have encountered too many business owners over the past few decades that came to me overworked and underpaid. The first thing I look at when increasing ARPC is whether my client is charging enough for their service. You would be surprised how many times I see entrepreneurs charging half of what their clients would eagerly pay to solve their problem or achieve their desire.

I learned this lesson for myself the hard way. When I started out, I only understood how to create value through discounting prices. I looked around the market and set my pricing at or below the competition. The problem with a discount pricing strategy is that you can discount yourself into bankruptcy.

Once I finally realized the true value of what I offer my clients, my rates rose as much as 600% in some cases. The unexpected outcome from raising my prices was my clients started to appreciate my service more, respected what I delivered, and therefore were more apt to implement my strategies properly and succeed.

If you are going through the first run of The Rule of 26, just increasing your prices by 26% could be the fastest and easiest way to meeting your first objective. Please note, that it will be difficult to make this change with your current clients without building more value to what you currently offer them.

I do however suggest working on getting everyone paying your new rates quickly after making the change. Otherwise, you risk losing interest in serving your grandfathered clients over your new, more profitable, and engaged clients.

A strategy that worked very well for Erica, a graphic designer I work with, is to redesign your product offering. Erica was offering a flat monthly fee for graphic design. There were certain stipulations to the various levels of service which kept her offerings profitable enough for her while providing great value to her clients. The rub came when Erica's lowest price tier became 70% of her business.

When working with a tiered flat rate pricing strategy, you gain a lot of simplicity in the sales, but risk what my client ran into. With 70% of Erica's clients taking advantage of her lowest tier package, she only had 30% of her available time to offer her higher tier services. This limits her earning potential. Of course, she could just hire more designers, but that meant more overhead, paperwork, and company structure than she wanted to take on. Since 70% of her business was paying on the lowest margin service, she couldn't risk jacking up the prices overnight.

Erica decided to restructure her lowest tier with a list of new benefits and bump the cost by about 30%. Instead of increasing the existing client's rate immediately, she told them that they were automatically upgraded to the new tier structure at the same rate through the end of their next billing cycle. So, if they were in month two of the current quarter, their rate wouldn't increase for four months.

She also gave them an option to bump their monthly or quarterly subscriptions to an annual term. This option postponed their rate increase up to 23 months. Erica's strategy proved to work extremely well. With the increased cash flow in annual subscriptions, she was able to invest in workflow and order request automation allowing her to take on more clients without sacrificing quality or begrudging the grandfathered subscribers.

Bundling

I understand that you can't always increase your current rate overnight. There are many aspects that go into individual industry pricing structures. When increasing your pricing isn't an option, you can create huge value by creating bundles of your popular services. Think of bundling multiple services in a series over time rather than an 'all at once' experience. You can also create bonus services or maybe even products related to your service to increase value. The more you bundle, the more value you create and in return, bill more.

One of my bundling stories is a water delivery service. They are in Anchorage Alaska where the tap water is sourced from a glacier fed lake. If you haven't had glacier fed lake water, you are missing out. Unfortunately, this meant my client had a reduced pool of potential clients. I mean, why would you pay for bottled water if the tap water was always cold, never hard, and crystal clear.

Fortunately for them, a few parts of town still have iron water pipes which deliver water with remnants of rusty and cloudy water. These perfect clients are mainly located downtown in commercial office buildings. Now what is just as prevalent as a water cooler in an office environment? You guessed it, coffee.

My water heroes originally came to me with an increasing cost of new client acquisition issue.

Working through their options, we discovered they could easily deliver coffee supplies along with water orders. Working with a local coffee roaster they were able to bundle the water, coffee, and coffee supplies delivery services. Bundling services saved their clients time, energy, and money while providing my client a drastic boost in revenue.

The magic of the bundling strategy came from selling a new service to existing clients which always cost less to convert than new prospects. What related services are you currently not offering that could easily be included with your existing services?

A hidden benefit of my water hero's new bundling options is more content on their website. More service options give visitors more to engage with, directly affecting the site's conversion rate. Win-win-win for everyone.

Upsell & Cross-Sell

For most professional salespeople, the art of the upsell is what separates the kids from the adults. For service-based businesses, offering a done-for-you version of a do-it-yourself program, or a mastery class, or maybe even one-to-one time with the expert are all great upsells. The upsell usually happens during the initial purchase, but you can find ways to get existing clients to upgrade their current services as well.

Upselling and cross-selling are almost second nature for my insurance and financial services clients. Vehicle insurance pays well, but the bigger ticket services lie with life insurance and retirement planning; this is where cross-selling comes in and the key is relationships.

Look beyond your clients' immediate service requirements and learn more about them as a person. Building a deeper relationship will give you more opportunities to identify other services you can offer them. My philosophy is that if you stay in tune with your client as a person and can identify their needs, you will never have to sell anything. Instead, you will become, in their eyes, a problem solver. People seek out problem solvers, which then alleviates ever having to sell your services. With current clients, my upsells and cross sells are merely identifying solutions to needs they bring to me, rarely the other way around.

Exclusivity & Scarcity

Another tactic to build value and increase revenue is to offer less. Elite access to you or early access to your next event creates a tremendous value to your customers. Exclusivity creates a premium of which you can bill say, 26% more for. Almost anyone can create a loyalty program. On the other hand, building an elite inner circle of raving fans that will pay top dollar to be the first or one of the few with access is priceless.

Coaches are well-known for exclusivity offers. One of my past coaching clients teaches people how to sell from the stage. This power-couple team brings people to a seminar on how to sell from a stage and literally just walks them through their own process while selling over 60% of the attendees on a $15,000 group coaching program. If that wasn't enough, they then offer five slots to additional one-to-one in-person coaching sessions with them for another $5,000.

This strategy is technically an upsell, but the value is built in the exclusivity mixed with scarcity. Would it have been worth $5,000 if they offered to everyone? Probably not. And while in these one-to-one sessions, the couple builds so much more value that their inner-circle students almost always buy whatever is offered to them next.

Offering your services to a limited number of people at a time builds tremendous value, especially if you have a reputation for being the best at what you do. Personalized services are a great fit for scarcity because they are usually time consuming for the service provider. The higher ticket price allows the entrepreneur to do what they love without having to service clients 52 weeks a year.

One of my fashion consulting clients, Mickela, charges an upward of $10,000 to come to your house, throw out most of your old clothes, and then go on a shopping spree to stuff your closet with attire that best suits your body type, skin color, and attitude. She is extremely good at what she does, but the process takes a lot of her energy, so she only offers to serve a limited number of clients per year. Some might say she charges too much, but the service is so impactful, she receives referrals from over 80% of her clients immediately after they complete her program. Mickela's pricing stratgey marries 'exlusivity' and 'billing what you are worth' to create a workload that serves her lifestyle. Charging more per client means she needs to serve less clients; allowing her to spend more time with her child and husband.

Intrinsic Value

You don't always have to increase the amount of time or produce more of anything to increase the value of your service. Establishing the value of time, energy, and money you save or create for your client increases the perceived value of what you have to offer. Portray this value on your website as much as possible. Use charts, graphs, or infographics to illustrate all the ways the client gains time, reduces effort, or earns more money by using your services. If you have a luxury centric business, your key is to help website visitors feel the quality or realize the prestige your service offers. In either case, a picture is worth a thousand words, so use them to your benefit in any way you can.

As you can see, increasing your average revenue per client depends less on digital strategy and more on your ability to bill for what you are worth and deliver on the promise of that value. Following through on our promises is the key to successfully increasing your ARPC and will define the longevity of your business. Your reputation is all you have, so be sure to under-promise and over-deliver every chance you get.

APPLYING THE RULE OF 26

Now that we have all the information we need to apply the Rule of 26, it's time to act. But where to start? For the best results, it is best to focus on one KPI at a time which keeps the process simple to manage while still increasing revenue as you crush objectives along the way. Remember, if you increase any *one* of the three metrics (unique visitors, converstion rate, or ARPC) by 26%, you increase your revenue by 26% and the workload that comes with it.

In my experience, it is best for service-based businesses to experience measured growth compared to instantaneously exploding their client list. This is especially true if you have an involved onboarding process for new clients. Taking a little time to accept and adapt to an increased client load will pay dividends in the end. Applying the Rule of 26 one KPI at a time gives you that kind of growth trajectory. Instead of eating the entire elephant in one bite, we work to increase revenue in increments.

With all that said, the growth trajectory between objectives *is* exponential. Reaching your first objective will increase revenue by 26%. Achieving the second objective increases your revenue 58% comparative to where you started. This leaves a 42% relative jump in revenue between objective two and three. That last jump gives you the 100% revenue growth the Rule of 26 promises along with the biggest jolt in workload.

These numbers are exciting, but we are still left with the question of where to start. The answer will be different for everyone. Here are common scenarios that can help you make the best decision for your business.

Low To No Traffic

If your traffic is less than 500 visits per month, the answer is clear; you need more traffic to your website. Here is the caveat: If you are getting less than 1,000 visitors to your website, don't settle for a 26% increase. In this case, I suggest shooting to get your unique monthly visitors to at least 1,000. A thousand unique visitors will give you enough traffic to establish a statistically measurable conversion rate and enough interactions for significant sales increase.

A common scenario is 50% of small businesses get less than 500 visitors a month to their website[6]. Reaching 1,000 unique visitors might seem significant, but it is just the tip of the iceberg. You must realize that a vast majority of visitors will be unqualified to work with you, which is why the average conversion rate for most industries lies below 2.35%[13].

Good Traffic No Calls

If you are getting at least 1,000 visitors a month, but getting little to no calls, you have a conversion problem. Even if your website attracts 10,000 visitors per month, but your conversion rate is below 2.35%, you still have a conversion problem.

Keep in mind that there is no reason for huge changes to your website unless you're seeing less than a 1% conversion rate. In all other cases, make calculated and incremental changes. Remember, we are only looking for tenths of a percentage point in increases here. Also keep in mind that this objective comes with a little mystery, so be patient.

Can't Handle More Sales

I am always skeptical when talking to entrepreneurs who tell me that they are so busy they couldn't possibly handle more clients or sales calls. Mainly because they often follow that statement with a complaint about how they are overworked or not bringing home enough in profits.

In business, being busy isn't a clear marker of success. I know from personal experience. When I started my business, there was only me and one part-time employee. At the end of my first year, I had recorded a dozen albums, a slew of smaller projects and built a large portfolio of graphic design projects. I worked 16 to 18-hour days, six to seven days a week for a solid year. I logged a whopping $72,000 in sales that year. My W-2 wages showed $23,000, my credit cards were at 80% of their limits, and I was tired.

I didn't have the margins to hire help and I didn't have any more time in the day to take on more clients, let alone more sales calls. Something had to change because this wasn't what I had in mind when I started my company.

If this sounds at all familiar, you need to look at your ARPC immediately. This situation isn't healthy for you or your business, so it's imperative that you change how you bill for your services sooner than later.

Conversion Rate High – Close Rate Low

A high conversion rate isn't always a sign of a profitable website. A day full of answering emails and calls from unqualified prospects is torture for anyone. Therefore, quality of your conversions is just as important as the quantity of leads from your website.

The average close rate for the service-based business is 20%[16]. If you fall below this mark, you have one of two problems. One, your sales process needs work. I am not the sales guru, so you will need to get another book for that issue. Number two possible issue is that the quality of your conversions is lacking.

If you fall into category two, go back to the Increasing Conversion Rates chapter, and read it through the lens of increasing the quality of your leads over the quantity.

None Of The Above

If your company's situation doesn't fit into any of these scenarios, then you have a unique situation. I love unique situations and I accept your challenge. Email me at buzz@buzzworthy.biz and I will personally help you decide where to get started with a complimentary one-to-one consult.

Rinse & Repeat

The Rule of 26 is so powerful because there is an infinite number of ways to achieve each goal due to the individuality between businesses. Though there are general strategies everyone will utilize, each journey will look different. So how you earn your 26% increase in unique traffic, conversion rate, and average revenue per client will be unique to you.

Once you double the revenue generated from your website using the Rule of 26, you are ready for phase two, Rinse & Repeat. As seen in figure two on the next page, applying the Rule of 26 a second time is extremely practical. Many times, Rinse & Repeat is easier because you have better cash flow to accelerate your goals for the second phase. As Alec Baldwin once touted, "Success begets success."

Using our original example numbers, you can see the Rule of 26 doesn't change and the numbers are still obtainable. It won't take much advertising to garner 655 more visitors per month and a 3.97% conversion rate is still well below the upper echelon of top converting websites.

The challenge of Rinse & Repeat comes with increasing your ARPC by 26% again. The objective will require a little more creativity the second time through and may take a bit longer to accomplish that the first time around. Just remember that your newer ARPC is your new standard. Forget that you have recently increased prices and approach Rinse & Repeat much like you did the first time around.

After the Rule of 26	Website Metric	Rinse & Repeat
2,520	Unique Visitors	3,175
3.15%	Conversion Rate	3.97%
$1,260	Average Revenue Per Client	$1,587.60
$100,018.80	Revenue	$200,113.01

Figure 2: Rinse & Repeat by the numbers

An alternative to increasing ARPC during Rinse & Repeat is to increase your traffic by 59%; meaning increasing traffic by 26% twice more. You're simply replacing ARPC with the second 26% increase in traffic. Using the example in figure two, once you have increased unique visitor traffic to 3,175, you will work to increase traffic again by 26% to 4,000. This strategy will likely require paid tactics but will be easier than doing the same with your conversion rate.

WRAP UP

Wow! We just covered a lot of information in a relatively short time. I encourage you to read through this entire book again and then each section multiple times as you start implementing the Rule of 26. I kept this book short on purpose, but there are many layers within everything I covered, so look past the surface of the content and look deep into your individual situation.

As you re-read this book, don't be afraid to let your mind wander on each point and write down everything that comes to your mind. Your imagination may surprise you. Remember to keep things as simple as you can. The more complex strategies you derive, the more that can go wrong. That's why simplicity is what the Rule of 26 is all about.

This book is by no means an exhaustive resource covering all the ways you can increase each of the three core website metrics mentioned. My intent is to give you a starting point and then have you run with the rule at will. Like I tell my clients on a regular basis, "there are many ways to make a peanut butter and jelly sandwich".

I often get asked how long it takes to be successful with the Rule of 26. The answer, of course, depends on many factors such as your time commitment, budget, current market environment, and competition to name a few. The Rule of 26 isn't a herculean effort, but there are also extraordinarily little in the way of shortcuts. Regardless of how you approach this journey, be patient with yourself, your marketers, and trust in the process.

Your patience will be tested mostly because marketing isn't a fast game. Success is usually incremental and measured over months, quarters, and years. As I mentioned earlier in the book, measured growth is a good thing. It allows you time to adjust your internal processes as you increase your client load. And believe me, your business *will* change by the time you double your revenue, so this time will be crucial to sustaining your success.

Trust in the process will come naturally as you immediately realize the fruits of your labor. Say you start with increasing traffic and you have a steady conversion rate. As traffic increases you will see an increase in inquiries. Same goes with increasing your conversion rate. All three objectives will give you some level of instantaneous results. The magic comes when the rule leverages your efforts as you progress from objective one to two and then the big jump by accomplishing the third.

The underlying gifts the Rule of 26 gives you are liberty, clarity, and knowledge. Liberty to ignore all the advertisements on your social media feed selling you on the next best marketing shortcut. Clarity in knowing that website marketing doesn't have to be complicated and that you now have a clear path to significantly increasing your revenue. The knowledge that you can drastically grow your business in a healthy and sustainable manner.

Now you have some choices to make. In the next chapters, I will review next steps, frequently asked questions, and share some helpful resources for your journey towards doubling your website revenue.

PART 3

THE NEXT STEP

THE NEXT STEP

Congratulations, you now know how to streamline your website marketing by only focusing on three key performance indicators. I hope you now realize how straightforward getting your website to produce more revenue can be. I also hope this inspires you to act and dive into the Rule of 26 immediately.

I wrote this book to be a starting point for your website marketing journey. As I see it, you have four opportunities in front of you.

1. You can close this book and keep doing what you have been doing, getting the same results from your website as you were before we started. If you have read this far though, I am sure this won't be the case.

2. You can start leveraging the Rule of 26 on your

own using the strategies and tactics I have outlined in this book.

3. If you have one, you can call your digital marketing team and try to get them to adopt the Rule of 26 and streamline your website revenue growth.

4. You can schedule a Rule of 26 strategy meeting with me to discuss the next steps to your website marketing success. There is no obligation and scheduling is super easy, so what do you have to lose? We'll never know whether we were meant to work together or not if we don't meet. Visit www.ruleof26.com to schedule this complimentary consult. I promise that you will leave the conversation with valuable insights. Regardless of whether we work together or not, I want the best for your business.

The options are yours to choose. I know progress can be scary sometimes, but we can never grow unless we act. Your business can't flourish if you don't take the steps necessary to propel it to the next level. If I can be of service, we can take that step together.

FREQUENTLY ASKED QUESTIONS

"Buzz, Why Don't I Just Increase My Traffic By 100% To Double My Website Revenue?"

Increasing your website traffic by 100% may double your website revenue, but then, maybe not. It is my experience that most service-based business websites are not converting at a high enough rate nor achieving the best ARCP. Merely stuffing 100% more traffic through your website leaves a lot of opportunity on the table. If you are paying for the added traffic, you are wasting a lot of money as well.

The Rule of 26 isn't designed to just double your

revenue. It also designed to be a website revenue optimizer. Maximizing the quality of all three objectives within the Rule of 26 optimizes your time and resources, which in returns makes you more profitable. And why bleed time, energy, and money with increasing just one KPI by 100% when you can leverage the Rule of 26, which only requires a combined 78% increase across three KPIs for the same results. In my opinion, it's better to work smarter, not harder.

"How Does The Rule Of 26 Work If I Don't Have Any Traffic Coming To My Website Right Now?"

The Rule of 26 works even if you recently launched your website or have a website that hasn't seen much love. Granted, you won't be working with the raw 26% increases we have covered in this book, but actions you take will have the same effect. If you are new to website marketing, I strongly urge you to reach out to me and let's find the best way for you to start getting some ROI from your website sooner than later. Let's face it; the longer you wait to establish an effective website presence, the more time, energy, and money you are wasting with little or no return.

"I Get Plenty Of Business From Sources Other Than My Website, So Why Should I Bother With Website Marketing?"

Website marketing is not the only way to grow a service-based business. It is, however, the most efficient way to increase quality leads and double revenue. In the early years, I too thought I was outperforming my website with networking, top of mind advertising, and other tactics. About five years into running my business, I finally stopped to analyze the numbers and quickly realized I was under-utilizing a powerful asset.

Effective websites are a business's spokesperson 24 hour a day, seven days a week, 365 days a year. It never takes a break, doesn't ask for a raise, and never calls in sick. Compare that to the amount of networking events available in a week and other sales exercises a human can spend their time with and you quickly see a clear winner. Remember, 68% of all transactions starting with an Internet search[12], your website is the most effective prospecting tool.

If you have a sales team, you owe it to yourself to leverage your website. A sales force can only make so many cold calls, knock on so many doors, and attend so many networking events. Leveraging your website can create a stream of inbound sales they can handle will reduce burnout and possibly the amount of salespeople you need to have on payroll. Reducing your sales staff by just one while garnering higher sales creates a huge swing in profitability.

"How Do I Know The Rul Of 26 Will Work For Me?"

When I set out to simplify the process of creating digital strategies for small and medium sized businesses, I wanted to make sure it could work for any kind of business, anywhere in the country. A surefire way to make something absolute is to use math, so that is what I did. The Rule of 26 is a mathematically backed strategy. Every angle of this simple rule is structured to leverage your time, energy, and money in a profitable manner.

There is no fluff in the Rule of 26. If you do the work, you *will* get the results. There are no two ways about it. Increase each KPI by 26% and see a 100% increase in the revenue you garner from your website traffic.

"What If I Don't Currently Have A Website?"

If you don't have a website, then you are definitely behind the curve, but not out of luck. The good news is that you know where to start, get a website. The other good news is that websites don't cost as much as they did just a few years ago.

There are many routes you can take when getting started with a website. You could build one yourself, work in tandem with a freelancer, or you can hire a professional website developer to do it for you. I have been working with website development since 1999; yes, I know I just dated myself. I have seen just about every scenario you can imagine. All three routes have advantages and drawbacks. All of which, I relate to home improvement scenarios.

Building a website on our own is like tackling a room remodel in your home. You get inspired by a show on HGTV or some other home improvement show and say to yourself, "How hard could it be?"

Getting started with demolition is easy enough until the unforeseen obstacles are uncovered, and the entire project becomes an out-of-control behemoth. At some point, you are force to bring in the calvary and hire a professional to finish what you started. In the end, everything works out, but there was a lot of headache to get there.

If you have little to no experience with design or website development, doing it yourself will be exceedingly difficult, but not impossible. Just know that you don't know what you don't know. If you can afford it, I urge you to at minimum work in tandem with a freelancer.

Using a freelancer to build a website is much like being your own general contractor for a large home project. Yes, you have professionals at your disposal, but they are working at your direction. If you steer the project awry, you the time and money for the freelancer to get you back on course. I only suggest this scenario if you have experience working with subcontractors and/or project management.

Hiring a website development firm is like hiring a general contractor to get everything done for you. Yes, this is the seemingly easy route, but it is the most expensive of your choices. But expense is relative if you consider the time you save trying to figure it out yourself and the quality you get when you work with a true professional.

In the end choosing your route will depend on your budget of time and money. If you have more time than money, you will most likely choose DIY or a done-with-you solution. If you have more money than time or lack the patience to figure it out on your own, go with hiring a professional website developer.

When looking for professionals to work with, make sure you vet them thoroughly. The cheapest route isn't always the best route, so don't get caught up with price as much as experience and portfolios. You professional should be willing to explain he process in a way you are comfortable. Remember, this is *your* website and *your* path to doubling your business's revenue, so you must be satisfied with the end result.

HELPFUL RESOURCES

➤ My company, Buzzworthy Integrated Marketing, offers several website marketing options that help business owners increase traffic and conversions. Visit www.buzzworthy.biz for more details.

➤ If you're tackling SEO on your own, there are a few options to choose from. My biased suggestion is Dizyo, but not just because it's one of my company's DIY marketing platforms, but because it simplifies the SEO process in a way the layman can execute SEO immediately. There are other options, which I have included in the list below, each with varying levels of complexity.

- www.dizyo.biz
- www.aioseo.com
- www.semrush.com
- www.ahrefs.com

➤ Other great books on how to both grow and optimize your business include:

- *The E-Myth Revisited* by Michael Gerber
- *Profit First* by Mike Michalowicz
- *Start With Why* by Simon Sinek
- *Just F*cking Do It: Stop Playing Small.* by Noor Hibbert
- *Live It, Love It, Sell It* by Jules White

- *Purple Cow* by Seth Godin
- *Selling the Invisible* by Harry Beckwith

If you are looking for any other resources, feel free to email me at buzz@buzzworthy.biz and I will do my best to get you pointed in the right direction.

ABOUT MICHAEL BUZINSKI

Michael "Buzz" Buzinski has been dubbed a visionary marketer by the American Marketing Association for thought leadership in digital marketing. He garners great satisfaction from helping entrepreneurs avoid the time drain and frustration of managing profitable digital marketing campaigns.

Michael has owned several businesses over the years. His first taste of entrepreneurialism came at the age of seven picking up walnuts off his parent's small farm and selling them to his Grandfather for $1.25 per gunny sack. Gross sales for the first season were $40; just enough money to buy Christmas presents for his parents and sister.

Since then, he has owned many ventures including a photography service, recording studio, media production studio, part owner of a professional indoor football team (Alaska Wild), café, and his integrated marketing firm.

Buzz has been managing the marketing needs for businesses and non-profit organizations since 1999. He has worked with over 750 brands including Bass Pro Shop, TGI Friday's, American Lung Association, AllState Insurance, Taco Bell, The YWCA, and Windows by Anderson just to name a few.

Along with being a serialpreneur, Buzz enjoys volunteering his time to several causes. He has sat on the board of directors for various small and large nonprofits such as the Alaska Air Museum, Alaska University Foundation, and National Information Technology committee for the Employer Support of Guard and Reserve.

Along with being a life-long learner, Michael is a devoted teacher and mentor. He offers time to mentor new vetrepreneurs (military veterans who separate from service and start a business) through the Warrior Rising program. He also frequently teaches workshops for the U.S. Small Business Administration and the Small Business Development Center along with keynote speaking engagements for various local and national industry associations.

On the personal side, Michael is a third-generation US Air Force Veteran. A failed professional musician, Buzz enjoys playing many instruments in his spare time. He enjoys telling dad jokes to his three nieces and six nephews and loves to travel around the world with his lovely wife, Heather, whenever their busy schedules allow.

BUZZWORTHY INTEGRATED MARKETING

Buzzworthy Integrated Marketing is a full-service website development and digital marketing firm. Focused on the needs of service-based businesses, Buzzworthy offers several levels of engagement from Do-It-Yourself digital marketing software platforms to white-glove Done-For-You services.

Buzzworthy's mission is to simplify the digital marketing process for small to medium sized businesses. Their 'choose your own adventure' model allows the client to decide how much or little Buzzworthy is involved with the marketing process. Business owners have the flexibility to customize their experience and integrate Buzzworthy to the best of their advantage.

Michael Buzinski, the company's founder, and CEO believes that small and medium sized businesses are the backbone to the American economy and the key to restoring the once thriving middle class our country so desperately needs to prosper. His vision is to leverage best-in-class digital marketing tools and proven strategies in ways small to medium sized businesses can afford, enabling them to compete with enterprise goliaths.

For more information visit www.buzzworthy.biz.

SMALL FAVOR

I am always interested to hear about how The Rule of 26 worked for readers. Please email me directly at buzz@buzzworthy.com. What worked best for you? What challenged you? How has the increased revenue helped your business and your life? What questions do you have? Let me know.

How did you enjoy this book? Please leave an honest review so others can benefit from your feedback. I personally check every review looking for insightful feedback.

Visit: www.Ruleof26.com/review

ACKNOWLEDGEMENTS

I first want to acknowledge my beautiful wife for believing in me and giving me the space to create this book. Her work in revolutionizing how history is taught by changing how information is shared inspired me to finish this project.

Thank you, to my father for continually giving me the space to be whatever I wanted to be. Over the years, you supported all my seemingly crazy exploits. From my budding want-to-be rock star days to my first full-time entrepreneurial venture, you encouraged me to chase my dreams. I want you to know how much it has meant to me.

I also want to recognize every entrepreneur who has trusted in me to help them market their business. Each of you has impacted me, inspired me, taught me, and built me into the marketer I am today. Without the experience I garnered from each of you, I wouldn't be writing this book.

Last, but not least, I acknowledge all the insight my peers have given me along the way. This includes every one of you that was in a mastermind, retreat, or the like with me. For those who sat around campfires or hung out in tiny hole-in-the wall bars contemplating world domination with me. You all know who you are, and I want you to know, I will never forget your impact on my life. If it were not for you, the Rule of 26 wouldn't exist.

GLOSSARY

ARPC: Average revenue per client is the gross revenue garnered from the business relationship during a set amount of time, be it monthly or annually.

Click-To-Call: Also known as click-to-talk or click-to-dial, CTC allows users to connect with a company by phone by clicking a phone number hyperlink on a website using a cellular or soft phone.

CMO: Chief Marketing Officer is a C-level corporate executive responsible for the overall marketing activities in an organization.

Conversion Rate: The rate at which unique visitors become leads from a website. To decipher a conversion rate, divide the number of leads the company receives by the number of unique visitors. e.g., 10 leads from 100 unique visitors equals a 10% conversion rate.

CRM: Customer Relationship Management is a technology (usually a sofware program) for managing all your company's relationships and interactions with current and potential clients.

CTA: Call to Action, (in advertising material) a piece of content intended to induce a viewer, reader, or listener to perform a specific act, typically taking the form of an instruction or directive (e.g., buy now or click here).

KPI: A Key Performance Indicator is a measurable value that demonstrates how effectively a company is achieving key business objectives. Organizations use KPIs at multiple levels to evaluate their success at reaching targets.[2]

Metadata: depicts hidden HTML elements that directly convey and simplify website information for search engines, performing an important part in successful Search Engine Optimization.

Mobile Responsive: website design with flexible layouts, images that responds to the user's screen size and orientation and changes the layout accordingly.

PPC: Pay-Per-Click is primarily used in social media and search engine advertising. The advertiser elects to only pay when a user clicks on the advertiser's advertisement.

ROI: An acronym for return on investment. an estimated measure of an investment's profitability above and beyond the initial investment.

SEO: Search engine optimization is the discipline of getting website pages to rank higher on search engine result pages.

SMB: Small and medium sized enterprises are normally considered for-profit organizations up to 250 employees.

Vetrepreneur: A military veteran who organizes and manages a business enterprise.

UX: An acronym that stands for "User Experience" and refers to the experience the user has when navigating a website.

BIBLIOGRAPHY

[1] US Small Business Administration, Frequently Asked Questions, *Small businesses comprise what share of the U.S. economy?*, September 2012, https://www.sba.gov/sites/default/files/FAQ_Sept_2012.pdf

[2] Klipfolio, *How to set actionable KPI Targets*, July 2017, https://www.klipfolio.com/blog/kpi-targets

[3] Chad Otar, Forbes Magazine, What Percentage Of Small Businesses Fail -- And How Can You Avoid Being One Of Them?, https://www.forbes.com/sites/forbesfinancecouncil/2018/10/25/what-percentage-of-small-businesses-fail-and-how-can-you-avoid-being-one-of-them/?sh=6cb8d30d43b5, Oct 25, 2018

[4] US Trade Representative, Issue by Issue Information Center, *Small- and Medium-Sized Enter-*

prises, *https://ustr.gov/trade-agreements/free-trade-agreements/transatlantic-trade-and-investment-partnership-t-tip/t-tip-12*

[5]Financial Samuri, The Average Homeownership Duration Is Too Short To Build Real Wealth, *https://www.financialsamurai.com/the-median-homeownership-duration-is-too-short-to-build-real-wealth*

[6]Search Engine Journal; Over 50% of Local Business Websites Receive Less Than 500 Visits Per Month, *https://www.searchenginejournal.com/over-50-of-local-business-websites-receive-less-than-500-visits-per-month/338137/#close*

[7]DMA Marketer, Marketer email tracker 2019, *https://dma.org.uk/uploads/misc/marketers-email-tracker-2019.pdf*

[8]Content Work, How to Calculate Email Subscriber Value – And Why You Should Care, *https://contentwonk.com/email-subscriber-value-2/*

[9]Oxford Languages, Call To Action, *https://languages.oup.com/google-dictionary-en/*

[10]K2 Agency, Facebook Reach in 2020: How many people see your posts?, *https://www.k6agency.com/blog/facebook-reach-2020/*

[11]Campaign Monitor, Ultimate Email Marketing Benchmarks for 2021: By Industry and Day, *https://www.campaignmonitor.com/resources/guides/email-marketing-benchmarks/*

[12] Si Quan Ong, 63 SEO Statistic for 2021, *https://ahrefs.com/blog/seo-statistics/*

[13] Geckoboard, Conversion Rates – Industry Benchmarks, *https://www.geckoboard.com/best-practice/kpi-examples/website-conversion-rate*

[14] Trips Reddy, How Chatbots Can Reduce Customer Service Costs by 30%, *https://www.ibm.com/blogs/watson/2017/10/how-chatbots-reduce-customer-service-costs-by-30-percent/*

[15] Sophia Bernazzani, How You Should Be using Chatbots for Customer Service, *https://blog.hubspot.com/service/customer-service-chatbots*

[16] Dan McDade, What Should the Sales Close Rate Be?, *https://www.prospect-experience.com/blog-gallery/2019/1/29/what-should-the-sales-close-rate-be*